Beautiful Birds

WOODPECKERS

By Kristen Rajczak Nelson

Gareth Stevens
PUBLISHING

Please visit our website, www.garethstevens.com. For a free color catalog of all our high-quality books, call toll free 1-800-542-2595 or fax 1-877-542-2596.

Library of Congress Cataloging-in-Publication Data
Names: Rajczak Nelson, Kristen, author.
Title: Woodpeckers / Kristen Rajczak Nelson.
Description: New York : Gareth Stevens Publishing, [2023] | Series: Beautiful birds | Includes index.
Identifiers: LCCN 2021035973 (print) | LCCN 2021035974 (ebook) | ISBN 9781538275320 (set) | ISBN 9781538275337 (library binding) | ISBN 9781538275313 (paperback) | ISBN 9781538275344 (ebook)
Subjects: LCSH: Woodpeckers–Juvenile literature.
Classification: LCC QL696.P56 R35 2023 (print) | LCC QL696.P56 (ebook) | DDC 598.7/2–dc23
LC record available at https://lccn.loc.gov/2021035973
LC ebook record available at https://lccn.loc.gov/2021035974

First Edition

Published in 2023 by
Gareth Stevens Publishing
29 East 21st Street
New York, NY 10010

Editor: Kristen Nelson
Designer: Andrea Davison-Bartolotta

Photo credits: Cover Harry Collins Photography/Shutterstock.com; p. 1 Seppo Miettinen/Shutterstock.com; p. 5 (bottom left) WolfPhotographie/Shutterstock.com; p. 5 (bottom right) Toukung design/Shutterstock.com; p. 5 (top left) Ondrej Prosicky/Shutterstock.com; p. 5 (top right) RaiPhoto/Shutterstock.com; p. 7 (bottom) Marcelo Morena/Shutterstock.com; p. 7 (top) Martin Pelanek/Shutterstock.com; p. 9 Karel Bock/Shutterstock.com; pp. 11, 24 (beak) J.A.Dunbar/Shutterstock.com; p. 13 C. Hamilton/Shutterstock.com; p. 15 Philip Rathner/Shutterstock.com; p. 17 Jamil Bin Mat Isa/Shutterstock.com; pp. 19, 24 (nest) Wang LiQiang/Shutterstock.com; pp. 21, 24 (egg) Rick & Nora Bowers/Alamy Stock Photo; p. 23 Mark Schocken/Shutterstock.com.

Printed in the United States of America

CPSIA compliance information: Batch #CSGS23: For further information contact Gareth Stevens, New York, New York at 1-800-542-2595.

Contents

Lots of Woodpeckers! 4
Pecking 10
Nesting Time 16
Babies! 22
Words to Know 24
Index. 24

Woodpeckers are birds. There are more than 180 kinds.

Most are black
and white.
Many have red or
yellow feathers too.

They live all over
the world.
They live in trees.

They have a
sharp beak.
They peck at wood.

They are looking
for bugs to eat.

Some eat fruit too.

They peck to
make nests.
It can take weeks.

The nests are holes.

Mothers lay eggs.
Eggs are white
and round.

Babies come out
of eggs.
They leave the nest in
about a month.

Words to Know

beak

egg

nest

Index

babies 22
colors 6
food 12, 14
pecking 10, 16